Alexander Hamilton

and the Founding of the Federal Government

Susan Bachner

Boston, Massachusetts
Chandler, Arizona
Glenview, Illinois
Upper Saddle River, New Jersey

Illustrations
2, 3, 6, 13 John White.

Photographs
Every effort has been made to secure permission and provide appropriate credit for photographic material. The publisher deeply regrets any omission and pledges to correct errors called to its attention in subsequent editions.

Unless otherwise acknowledged, all photographs are the property of Pearson Education, Inc.

Photo locators denoted as follows: Top (T), Center (C), Bottom (B), Left (L), Right (R), Background (Bkgd)

Opener: National Geographic Photographer-George F. Mobley/Courtesy of the U.S. Capitol Historical Society; 1 National Geographic Photographer-George F. Mobley/Courtesy of the U.S. Capitol Historical Society; 4 Library of Congress; 5 Ivy Close Images/Alamy; 7 National Archives; 8 National Geographic Photographer-George F. Mobley/Courtesy of the U.S. Capitol Historical Society; 9 The Federalist (vol. 1) J and A M'Lean, publisher, New York, 1788. From Rare Books and Special Collections Division in Madison's Treasures/Library of Congress; 10 Thinkstock; 11 Bureau of Engraving and Printing; 12 Federal Reserve Bank of San Francisco; 14 Library of Congress; 15 ©Caitlin Mirra/Shutterstock.

ISBN-13: 978-0-328-67697-2
ISBN-10: 0-328-67697-7

7 8 9 10 V0FL 16 15 14 13

A Boy from the Caribbean

In 1791, Alexander Hamilton was sworn in as the nation's first Secretary of the Treasury. He was the perfect choice for the job, with a sharp mind and an eye for details. Hamilton was ambitious, too. But unlike other leaders of the new nation, he did not come from a wealthy family. He was not even born in the country. Despite these obstacles, he became one of the founders of our country.

Alexander Hamilton was born in 1757 in the Caribbean island of Nevis. Soon after his birth, his family moved to St. Croix. When Alexander was still young, his father abandoned the family, leaving his mother Rachel to support young Hamilton and his brother. They were very poor and struggled to get by. Then Rachel died, and the two boys were left to care for themselves.

To provide for his brother, Hamilton began working for a businessman named Nicolas Cruger. Hamilton worked hard and studied every detail of Cruger's business, even writing reports about ways to save money.

Hamilton's ambition paid off. Cruger was impressed with his hard work and particularly with his writing skills. He and some other adults raised money and made plans for young Hamilton to get a good education in Britain's Thirteen Colonies.

Alexander had to support himself at a young age. He was very ambitious.

This drawing shows King's College in the 1700s. Today, King's College is Columbia University.

Hamilton arrived in the Thirteen Colonies in 1772 and attended one year of school in New Jersey. He had received no formal education in St. Croix and must have realized that he would have to work hard to keep up with the other students. Hamilton was driven to succeed. Every night he would read in his room until midnight. In the morning before school, he would study in a nearby cemetery.

The following year, Hamilton finished school and was admitted to King's College in New York City. He was now in one of the largest cities in the English-speaking world. New York was bustling with people. But most interesting to Hamilton were the debates about government.

At the time, the British government controlled the American colonies. Great Britain had been raising taxes on the American colonists to pay its war debts.

Revolution in the Air

There was much disagreement in New York about the British. **Loyalists** believed that to stay on good terms with Great Britain, colonists should pay the taxes even if they got little in return. **Patriots** thought the taxes and British control were unfair and many wanted to establish an independent nation.

People on both sides of the debate wrote pamphlets to hand out to people in the streets. The writers often used pseudonyms, or fake names, to avoid being attacked.

Hamilton disagreed with the Loyalists' views. He wrote two pamphlets of his own and signed them "A Friend to America." Hamilton's pamphlets were so well written that many people thought a well-known Patriot, John Jay, had written them.

New York City looked very different in the 1700s than it does today.

Hamilton Stops an Angry Mob

Even though he was a Patriot himself, Hamilton disliked it when mobs of Patriots attempted violent acts. He risked his life to take a stand against violence one night when angry revolutionaries showed up at the house of his college president, Myles Cooper, a Loyalist. Hamilton was bold and stood in front of Cooper's house to prevent the mob from getting in. Hamilton convinced the mob that harming Cooper would hurt their cause.

The Battle of Trenton, fought in 1776, was a great victory for General Washington and his troops.

The War Years

After being active in the Patriot cause in New York, Hamilton decided to join the fight for American independence. In 1775, he enlisted with a **military** drill company called the Corsicans. The company practiced marching together in a churchyard.

Soon enough, the time for practicing was over. War had begun in Boston, and it soon came to New York. In March 14, 1776, Hamilton entered the Continental Army as a captain.

Hamilton took charge and organized his own company of soldiers. He showed great bravery at the Battle of Trenton, where he and his men kept British troops from crossing the Raritan River and attacking George Washington's army.

Meeting George Washington

General George Washington heard about Hamilton's bravery and asked to meet him. Right away, Washington recognized Hamilton's leadership abilities and asked him to be his assistant. Hamilton was not yet 20 years old.

The meeting with Washington was the beginning of a long and important relationship. Washington liked Hamilton and saw that, like himself, Hamilton was thoughtful and logical in approaching a problem. In a short time, Hamilton became a trusted advisor to Washington. Just as he had helped improve in Nicolas Cruger's business years before, Hamilton studied how operations in the army could be improved and wrote reports to Washington about his findings.

During the cold winter of 1777–1778, Hamilton helped Washington plan strategies at Valley Forge. Though he enjoyed being an advisor to Washington, he still wanted the thrill of winning battles. So in 1781, Hamilton took command of an entire battalion.

As commander, Hamilton led an attack on a British fort in Yorktown and pressed the British troops there to surrender. He was promoted to the rank of colonel on September 30, 1783. By the end of the year, he left the military as a war hero.

Alexander Hamilton and George Washington met in 1777. Washington came to depend on Hamilton's brilliant mind.

After the War

On Dec. 14, 1780, Hamilton married Elizabeth Schuyler. She was a member of a prominent and wealthy New York family. Hamilton was an ambitious man, haunted by his poor upbringing. By marrying Elizabeth, he could rise into the ranks of New York society. The Hamiltons had a happy marriage. They raised eight children together.

This portrait of Elizabeth Hamilton was made in 1787. Elizabeth lived to be 97 years old.

After the war, Hamilton studied law and began working as a lawyer in 1782. Elizabeth's family connections brought him wealthy clients for his law practice. But he also took on cases defending Loyalists, the people who had sided with Britain before and during the war.

After the war, many lawmakers wanted to punish the Loyalists. They passed laws that stripped them of their rights and took away their money. But Hamilton believed that punishing the Loyalists would only hurt the new country. He saw the Loyalists as people who had a lot to offer the new nation. His defense of them was criticized by some. But it helped to establish the idea of equal treatment under the law. This is an important part of our legal system today.

A New Constitution

After winning the war against Britain, the states approved a new plan of government called the Articles of Confederation. But the Articles proved to be too weak, and gave too much control to the states. There was also no plan to pay off debts from the war. So in 1787, representatives from each state met in Philadelphia to revise the Articles. Instead, they wrote a new **constitution**.

Hamilton had ideas about what shape this new plan for government should take. He argued that the federal government should have power over the states. The interests of the nation, he said, were more important than the interests of each state. Unlike the other delegates, Hamilton had been born outside of the colonies. He had never developed loyalty to any one state. The other representatives did not agree with everything Hamilton said, but they agreed that the federal government needed more power. Hamilton's ideas helped shape the new government.

George Washington, shown standing on the right, led the Constitutional Convention. Also shown are Alexander Hamilton, Benjamin Franklin and James Madison.

The Federalist Papers

After the Constitution was drafted, Hamilton returned to face criticism from New Yorkers who did not want to give up control to a central government. When Hamilton's opponents attacked the Constitution, he tried to convince them to support it by writing letters to the newspapers under the name "Caesar." But the Caesar letters did not change a lot of minds.

Together with James Madison and John Jay, Hamilton then wrote what became known as the Federalist Papers. These were 85 essays that appeared in several New York newspapers. They explained the new Constitution and the powers of the President, the Congress, and the courts.

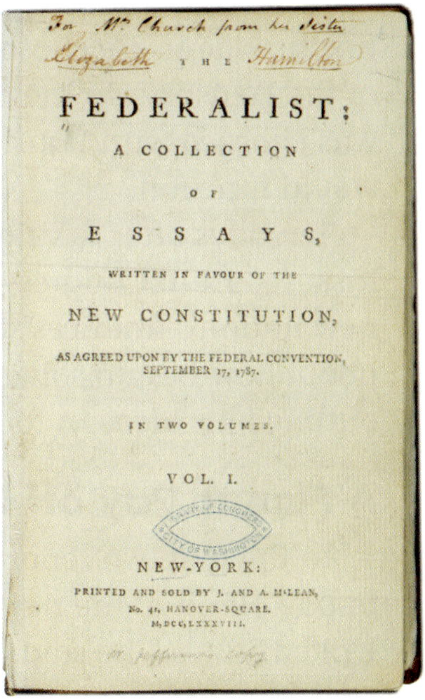

This is the title page of the first printing of the Federalist Papers. These essays were important in persuading New Yorkers and others around the country to support the new Constitution.

The Federalist Papers promoted **federalism**, the idea of a strong central government. This federal government would have power above that of the states. Thanks to the Federalist Papers, New Yorkers began to support the Constitution and eventually **ratified** it. As for Hamilton, he continued to promote federalism for the rest of his career.

The Treasury

In 1789, George Washington was sworn in as the nation's first president. He chose Alexander Hamilton to be Secretary of the Treasury. As the first Treasury Secretary, Hamilton was charged with figuring out how the new department would function.

Ten days after taking office, Hamilton was given his first task: report to Congress on how he was going to make the new nation's finances strong. Hamilton had thought a lot about how best to solve the country's money problems. He outlined his ideas in four important reports.

A Plan to Pay off Debt

In the first two reports, Hamilton laid out his plan to pay off all of the new nation's debt. "The debt of the United States," he said, "was the price of liberty." Feeding, clothing, and arming soldiers cost money, and each state had borrowed from wealthy Americans and foreign governments to pay for the war. Now the bills were due.

The Department of the Treasury is now located in the Treasury Building in Washington, D.C.

Alexander Hamilton is one of two people on U.S. paper money who was not a president. The other one is Benjamin Franklin.

When Hamilton proposed to pay the states' debts, many people disagreed with him. But Hamilton was practical. Paying one large debt, he reasoned, was more efficient than having each state pay its own.

How did Hamilton propose to pay these debts? A federal government must have a source of income. So Hamilton offered several ideas to raise money. He suggested a tax on imported goods and another tax on alcohol.

Many people were upset at the idea of taxes. After all, taxes were a main cause of the war with Britain. But there were few options. After much debate, Congress agreed with Hamilton's plan, and the debt was paid.

Hamilton's decision to pay the nation's bills was an important one. It gave other countries confidence in American businesses. And it gave the federal government a steady source of income—taxes. This income gave the federal government power over the states.

The first Bank of the United States issued paper money that had an agreed-upon value.

A Plan for a National Bank

In Hamilton's third report to Congress, he explained his idea for a national bank. The bank, according to Hamilton, would be a place where the Treasury would keep money collected from taxes and other sources of income. The Treasury could also borrow money from the bank. Likewise, individuals and companies could open accounts and borrow money, too.

The first Bank of the United States opened in December of 1791. Right away, the bank began to issue paper money. The new money was necessary because paper money issued by the states during the war was not worth anything. Now everyone had currency, or money, that had an agreed-upon value. The bank began lending money, which helped businesses to grow and helped make the nation's economy stronger.

A Plan to Protect American Businesses

In his last report to Congress, Hamilton laid out his plan to protect America's industries. He saw America's future not just in farming, but also in manufacturing. Through manufacturing, Hamilton believed that the United States could create jobs for its people as well as products that could be sold in the United States. This was important because it kept money within the country.

The best way to protect American companies from foreign competition, Hamilton argued, was **tariffs**. These were additional taxes on imported goods. Tariffs made imported products more expensive than goods made in the United States, encouraging people to buy American products. It was a strategy that helped to make the new country financially successful.

Life after the Government

Hamilton had fought bravely in a war. He had advised George Washington, signed the Constitution, and built the country's entire financial system. But now he was tired of politics. He retired from his official political life and started a newspaper, *The New York Evening Post,* which allowed him to continue to express his political ideas.

Hamilton's plan to protect American manufacturing helped many factories get started.

According to witnesses, Hamilton did not aim at Burr in the duel. Burr, on the other hand, shot directly at Hamilton.

Hamilton was no longer in public office, but many people still valued his opinion. In 1804, there was an election for the governor of New York. Many New Yorkers supported the country's vice president, Aaron Burr. Hamilton and Burr had long been political enemies, and Hamilton published articles supporting another candidate. Burr lost the election.

Burr was furious that Hamilton had campaigned against him. Soon after, Burr heard a rumor that Hamilton had called Burr a "dangerous man." It is not clear if the rumor was true, but it enraged Burr further. Determined to defend his name, Burr challenged Hamilton to a duel, a formal combat between individuals. Hamilton did not want to duel. But he felt he had no choice—it was a matter of honor.

On July 11, 1804, Alexander Hamilton faced Aaron Burr in a field in New Jersey. The two men fired their weapons. Hamilton's bullet hit a tree, but Burr's bullet found its target. Hamilton was wounded and died the next day. He was 47 years old.

Hamilton's Contribution

Hamilton was born into a poor family outside of the Thirteen Colonies. But by the time of his death, he was well-known in the United States. He had fought for his adopted country in the Revolutionary War. He was a voice for federalism, and he helped craft and defend the Constitution. Much of the structure of our government is the work of Hamilton.

Perhaps his most important contribution is the American financial system. As first Secretary of the Treasury, Hamilton realized that without enough money to back the government, the new country would fail. His plans for the Treasury Department were bold and far-sighted. While they kept the United States from financial failure, they also set it on a path for future greatness.

Alexander Hamilton is buried in Trinity Churchyard in Manhattan.

Glossary

constitution a written plan for government

federalism the belief in a strong central government

military having to do with the armed forces of a country

Loyalist a colonist who supported the British during the American Revolution

Patriot a colonist who supported the fight for American independence

ratify to give official approval, as to the Constitution or to amendments to it

tariff a tax on goods coming into a country